MW01195219

THE
FAMILY
THAT
CHANGED

THE FAMILY THAT CHANGED

A Child's Book About Divorce

by Francine Susan Spilke

Illustrated by Tom O'Sullivan

A HERBERT MICHELMAN BOOK

Crown Publishers, Inc.
New York

Printed in the United States of America

Published simultaneously in Canada by General Publishing Company Limited

Library of Congress Cataloging in Publication Data

Spilke, Francine Susan.
    The family that changed.

    (Her The divorced family)
    SUMMARY: Presents a brief explanation of what
happens to a family when a divorce occurs.
        1. Divorce—United States—Juvenile literature.
[1. Divorce] I. Title.   II. Series.
HQ834.S68 1979   301.42'84   79-16196
ISBN 0-517-53785-0

THE
FAMILY
THAT
CHANGED

Have you ever seen a new baby? It is so small, and it has such tiny feet and hands. You were once this small, with a little nose and mouth, and two tiny ears.

Everything living has to start growing. A cow and a bull start every little calf. A rooster and a hen start every little chick. And a man and a woman start every little baby. That is how you started too.

Once upon a time a nice man and a nice woman wanted to live together because they loved each other. The man and the woman liked to do all kinds of things together. They liked to go places together. They liked to dance together. They liked to go walking together in the park and hold hands. They were happy when they were together because they would laugh a lot. They liked to talk to each other and just wanted to be together all the time. The man thought the lady was special and the woman thought the man was special. So they got married. Before long the man and the woman wanted to have a baby. So they did.

You were the special baby they had. You were tiny and cuddly and they loved you very much. Now the woman was called the mommy and the man was called the daddy.

Like everything starting to grow, you were much too tiny to do a single thing for yourself. Every animal wants to take care of its babies. Dogs want to take care of their puppies. Cats want to take care of their kittens. Ducks want to take care of their ducklings.

And your mommy and daddy want to take care of you. They wanted to take good care of you when you were a baby, and they want to take good care of you now.

When you were a tiny baby, they wanted to feed you and play with you. They wanted to bathe you and hold you in their arms and hug you and kiss you. They would smile at you a lot, and you would smile back at them. They had fun watching you grow. Soon you could walk and talk and eat with a spoon and do all kinds of grown-up things. Your mommy and daddy were very proud of the things you could do.

You are not a baby anymore. You may already be three years old, maybe four, or you might even be as grownup as five or six. But even though you are not a baby, you are still growing all the time. You will be growing for many more years. Your mommy and daddy will want to take care of you and see to it that you have all the things a child needs to grow big and strong and happy.

You are very special to your mommy and daddy. They are very special to you. Your mommy and daddy will always care about what happens to you and each of them will try to do things for you in his and her own special way. Your mommy enjoys teaching you new things and your daddy enjoys helping you learn new things. They both still enjoy watching you grow and are very proud of the things you can do. Your mommy and daddy can still remember the first words you said, your first bath, your first steps, your first smile. Why don't you ask them and find out what they remember best?

Your mommy tries very hard to take care of you and has her own special way of doing things to make you happy. Your daddy also tries very hard to do things that will make you happy and he has his own special way of loving you and caring for you. A mommy and daddy do not always have to be together to do things for their child. There are many times that your mommy is with you and the two of you do all kinds of nice things together. There are many times that you may go places with only your daddy and the two of you do special things together.

Your mommy and daddy do not even have to be living together in the same house to take care of you and to do things with you and to love you just as much.

Your mommy or daddy bought this book for you because they want to tell you about something that is going to change in your family. This book will help them tell you about it.

Sometimes people who get married to each other cannot stay married to each other. They are no longer happy being together. They do not want to go dancing with each other anymore. They do not want to hold hands anymore. They do not even want to talk to each other all the time anymore. They stop feeling happy when they are together and they do not laugh anymore. Sometimes they may even quarrel and get angry at each other. They may shout a lot instead of talk, and they may not want to do things together anymore. Some of these things may be happening to your mommy and daddy. That is why they are not going to be living together in the same house anymore. One of them is going to be living someplace else. But one of them is still going to be living with you.

Your mommy and daddy are not going to be married to each other anymore. This is called getting a divorce. This means that either your mommy or your daddy is not going to be living with you in your home anymore. But you will still be living with one of them. If you live with your mommy you can still see your daddy. If you live with your daddy you can still see your mommy. When a mommy and daddy get a divorce, sometimes the daddy goes to live someplace else. Sometimes it is the mommy who goes to live someplace else. Your mommy and daddy will tell you just what is going to happen in your family.

But you are so very special and loved by your mommy and daddy that no matter what happens they will always want you and love you (and your sisters and brothers if you have any).

Nothing your mommy and daddy did for you will change because they are divorced. They will both still love you just as much as before. This will never change. They will still want to take care of you just as they do now.

Even though they will not be married to each other anymore, they will always be your mommy and daddy. Getting a divorce does not change that. You will always have your mommy and your daddy. Your mommy will still be your mommy. Your daddy will still be your daddy. They still care very much about you and will still want to do everything they can for you. They care very much about how you feel and will still want to do things to make you happy.

If your daddy is the one to be moving out, you will still be able to see him very often. If your mommy is the one to be moving out, you will still be able to see her very often. You do not lose your mommy or daddy because one of them does not live with you anymore. Your mommy or daddy will come to visit you often and you will still be able to do many things you did before. Your daddy will still take you to the park and to other places to have fun. He may even take you to see the place where he is living. He may buy a special bed to put in his new home for you to

sleep in and to stay with him sometimes if you would like that. Your mommy will still go shopping with you and take you to a friend's house to play.

Your mommy and daddy are not the only mommy and daddy to get a divorce. You may have other friends whose mommies and daddies have gotten a divorce. There are many children today who live with only one parent because their mommies and their daddies have gotten a divorce. Getting a divorce

does not mean that anyone has done anything wrong. Nothing bad is going to happen to you or to your mommy or your daddy. Your mommy is still the same woman that she was before. Your daddy is still the same man that he was before. And you are still the very lovable and special child you were before. No one will stop liking or loving you because your mommy and daddy are getting divorced. Your mommy and daddy have not done anything wrong. You have not done anything wrong. And your mommy and daddy are not getting divorced because of anything you have done. You have nothing to do with why they are getting divorced, and you cannot

do anything to change it. It is better to live with just a happy mommy or daddy all the time than to live with two unhappy parents. A divorce can make both your mommy and daddy happy again. They will probably be more fun to live with than they have been for a while.

Your mommy and daddy are getting a divorce because they are not happy living with each other anymore. But they are both still very happy that you are their child. They both still want you very much and each one of them would still like to be able to live with you. But it is not enough to love you and want you. They must see which one of them will be better able to take care of you and do all the things you need done for you. Someone must be able to cook the food for you to eat, wash your clothes, and take care of your home, keep it clean and neat, get you ready for school—if you go to school—and be home when you are not in school to look after you. Young children cannot do these things for themselves. They must have a grown-up to do them.

Your mommy and daddy will tell you which one of them you are going to live with. One thing you can be sure of—your mommy and daddy will make sure that no matter who you are living with, you will always be able to see both of them. Your mommy and daddy will not stop loving you or wanting to see you because one of them does not live with you anymore. They will still want to see you and love you just as much as ever.

You can be very happy because you still have a family. You will be happy doing things with your mommy . . .

and you will be happy doing things with your
daddy.